C000147305

# The Best Things in Life are Free

# The Best Things in Life are Free

## Lucy Duckworth

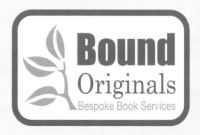

We think all laying hens deserve to enjoy natural freedoms whilst they lay tasty eggs for us to eat; that means freedom to roam on green pasture, freedom to enjoy sunshine, freedom to scratch for insects and freedom to lay an egg in a nest.

Here's what we do in a nutshell (or you could say eggshell):

- Each year we save approximately 60,000 hens from slaughter and find them caring pet homes through our network of regional centres so they can enjoy a free range retirement.

- We educate consumers about the caged eggs hidden in processed foods, like pasta, quiche, cakes and mayonnaise so they can make an informed choice when shopping.

- Our positive campaign style has been described as pioneering and one of our most successful campaigns was in persuading Hellmanns to produce a free range mayonnaise; as a result thousands of hens now enjoy freedom.

- We take hens at the end of their commercial laying life from almost 50 farmers around the UK all of whom support our work.

- We lobby MPs and MEPs to support British farmers and protect them from cheap imports where we have no control over welfare.

- We actively promote our Great British Free Range Farmer – there's a lot of happy hens free ranging the UK countryside because of their investment.

- We developed the original 'Eggsellence Award' given to eating establishments that use only free range eggs.

I'm youth, I'm joy,
I'm a little bird
that has broken
out of the egg.
J M Barrie (1860-1937)
Scottish dramatist

Our way is not soft grass, it's a hill path with lots of rocks. But it goes upwards, onwards, towards the sun.
Author unknown

To love
is the
great
amulet
that
makes
this
world
a garden.
Robert Louis Stevenson
(1850-1894)
Scottish novelist and poet

Gossip
is just
news
running
ahead of
itself in
a red
satin dress.
Liz Smith (b.1923)
American writer

There is
    an island
        of opportunity
in the
    middle of
        every difficulty.
English proverb

Where there is
great love
there are always
miracles.
Willa Cather (1873-1947)
American author

# All good things are wild and free.

Henry David Thoreau
(1817-1862)
American poet and philosopher

One should either
be a work of art
or wear a work of art.
Oscar Wilde (1854-1900)
Irish poet and playwright

Love flies,
   runs,
      and rejoices;
it is free
   and nothing
      can hold it back.
Thomas à Kempis (1379-1471)
German writer

Friendship is precious,
not only in the shade,
but in the sunshine of life.
Thomas Jefferson (1743-1826)
Former US President

# It is better to run back than run the wrong way.

English proverb

The garden suggests
there might be a place
where we can meet
nature halfway.
Chinese proverb

Where you will sit
when you are old
shows where you
stood in youth.
African proverb

You can't stop
the waves,
but you can
learn to surf.
Swami Satchidananda (1914-2002)
Indian religious teacher

# Flying is simple.
# You just throw yourself
# at the ground and miss.

Excerpt from 'So Long
and Thanks for All the Fish'
Douglas Adams (1952-2001)
English writer

Have nothing
in your house
that you do not
know to be useful,
or believe to
be beautiful.
William Morris (1834-1896)
Artist and social reformer

A journey
of a thousand miles
begins with a single step.
Lao Tzu (600 BC-531 BC)
Chinese Taoist philosopher

**Beauty is
not in the face;
beauty is
a light in the heart.**
Kahlil Gibran (1883-1931)
American philosopher and poet

What is life? It is the flash of a firefly in the night. It is the breath of a buffalo in the wintertime. It is the little shadow which runs across the grass and loses itself in the sunset.

Crowfoot (c.1830-1890)
Chief of the Siksika First Nation

Coming together
is a beginning.
Keeping together
is progress.
Working together
is success.

Henry Ford (1863-1947)
American industrialist

**Childhood
is the most beautiful
of all life's seasons.**
Author unknown

The block of granite
which was an obstacle
in the pathway of the weak
becomes a stepping-stone
in the pathway of the strong.
Thomas Carlyle (1795-1881)
Scottish historian and essayist

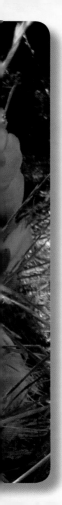

Rest is not idleness,
and to lie sometimes
on the grass on a
summer day listening
to the murmur of water,
or watching the clouds
float across the sky,
is hardly a waste of time.
Sir John Lubbock (1834-1913)
English politician and banker

Sister to sister
we will always be,
A couple of nuts
off the family tree.
Author unknown

Keep a green tree
in your heart
and perhaps
a singing bird
will come.
Chinese proverb

Marriage brings
   out the animal
      in some men
         —usually the chicken.
Author unknown

Rejoice with
your family
in the beautiful
land of life.
Albert Einstein (1879-1955)
Theoretical physicist

The flower
that follows
the sun does so
even on cloudy days.
Robert Leighton (1611-1684)
Scottish preacher

The man who removes a mountain begins by carrying away small stones.

Chinese proverb

Adopt the pace of nature;
her secret is patience.
Ralph Waldo Emerson (1803-1882)
American poet, lecturer and essayist

To love
and be
loved
is to feel
the sunshine
from
both sides.
Author unknown

Merrily, merrily
shall I live now,
Under the blossom
that hangs on the bough.
William Shakespeare (1564-1616)
English dramatist, playwright and poet

True friendship
can never be
broken; it can
only be tested.
Author unknown

# The best
## things
### in life
#### are free.
Englısh proverb

Sitting quietly,
doing nothing,
spring comes,
and the grass
grows by itself.
Zen saying

How does the Meadow flower its bloom unfold? Because the lovely little flower is free down to its root, and in that freedom bold.

William Wordsworth (1770-1850) English poet

## Picture Credits

Many thanks to those who kindly donated their pictures to this book.

Cover - © Dominic Coburn
Spine - © Nikki Scholes
Page 2 - © Exe Valley Eggs
Page 5 - © Sarah Willans
Page 6 - © Dave Cavill
Page 9 - © Dominic Coburn
Page 10 - © Elisabeth Aubury
Page 13 - © Lynnette Henderson
Page 14 - © Felix van de Gein
Page 17 - © Andy Garner
Page 18 - © Marko Marinović
Page 21 - © John Martin
Page 22 - © Joe Jackson
Page 25 - © Dawn Millholland
Page 26 - © Yani Wood
flickr.com/yanination
Page 29 - © Lisa Pope
Page 30 - © Nikki Scholes
Page 33 - © Jim Shields Photography
www.shields.org.uk
Page 34 - © Shannon Jade Jones
Page 37 - © Kate Farnady

Page 38 - © Bonnie Martin
Page 41 - © Courtesy of BHWT
Page 42 - © Jeroen François
Page 45 - © Sarah Tarrant
Page 46 - © Lisa Jordan
Page 49 - © Darren Wood
Page 50 - © Jane Howorth
Page 53 - © Meg Barlow-Hartley
and the Wharton Family
Page 54 - © Dominic Coburn
Page 57 - © Linda Bowman
Page 58 - © Exe Valley Eggs
Page 61 - © Jessica Cross
Page 62 - © Jane Butler
Page 65 - © Jim Shields Photography
www.shields.org.uk
Page 66 - © Joanna Hill
Page 69 - © Larissa Cozma
Page 70 - © Sophie Clarke
Page 73 - © Leigh Johnson
Page 74 - © Stéphane Bouguennec
Page 77 - © Francis Lopez
Page 80 - © Louise Mallinson

All copyrights of the photographic images are owned by the individual photographers who have kindly donated their image to this project. Every effort has been made to contact the current copyright holders. Any omission is unintentional and the publisher would be pleased to hear from any copyright holder not acknowledged.

## Text Credits

Excerpt from 'So Long and Thanks for All the Fish' by Douglas Adams, published by Pan Macmillan, London. Copyright © Douglas Adams, 2001

# The Best Things in Life Are Free
## 978-1-906181-09-3

Published by Bound Originals on behalf of the British Hen Welfare Trust
North Parks • Chulmleigh • Devon • EX18 7EJ • Tel: 01769 580310
info@bhwt.org.uk • www.bhwt.org.uk • Registered Charity No. 1109060

© Bound Originals 2011
Tithe Barn • Clouts Farm • Ide Hill Road • Bough Beech • TN8 7PH
www.boundoriginals.co.uk

No part of this publication may be reproduced, transmitted or stored in a retrieval system, in any form, or by any means without permission in writing from the publisher. This book is sold subject to the condition that it shall not, by way of trade or otherwise, be lent, hired out, resold, or otherwise circulated without the publisher's prior consent in any form or binding or cover other than that in which it is published, and without a similar condition being imposed on the subsequent purchaser.

10 9 8 7 6 5 4 3 2 1
1st Edition
Printed in China

To the best of the publisher's knowledge the inclusion of quotations in this compilation falls under the fair use or public domain guidelines of copyright law. If however, the publisher has inadvertently made any error they would be grateful for notification. Every effort has been made to contact the current copyright holders. Any omission is unintentional and the publisher would be pleased to hear from any copyright holder not acknowledged.

All copyrights of the photographic images are owned by the individual photographers who have kindly granted Bound Originals the right to use them for this publication.

Thank you for supporting the British Hen Welfare Trust.